Freedoms
After 50

Freedoms
After 50

Sue Patton Thoele

Foreword by Sandra Martz

Editor of
*When I'm An Old Woman I
Shall Wear Purple*

CONARI PRESS
Berkeley, California

Conari Press books are distributed by Publishers Group West.

ISBN: 1-57324-126-1

Cover design and illustration: Lisa Burnett Bossi,
Fineline Marketing & Design
Cover art direction: Ame Beanland
Interior design: Suzanne Albertson
Author photo: Paige Eden Thoele

Library of Congress Catalog-in-Publication Data
Thoele, Sue Patton.
Freedoms after 50 / Sue Patton Thoele :
foreword by Sandra Martz.
p.   cm.
ISBN 1 57324-126-1
1. Middle aged woman — Psychology.
2. Aged women — Psychology. 3. Self-actualization.
4. Autonomy (Psychology) I. Title.
HQ1059.4.T49   1998
305.244 — dc21   98-39638
CIP

Printed in the United States of America on recycled paper
99   00   01   02   RRD   10 9 8 7 6 5 4 3 2

When I was a young woman,
I thought aging meant loss and limitation,
but I've learned that it's really
about freedom.

With gratitude to all of the wonderful women
who have graced my life in both simple and profound
ways. For your love, comfort, laughter, and wisdom,
I thank you from the depths of my heart!

Freedoms After 50

After fifty, I am free to . . .

Foreword

Reading *Freedoms After 50* is like chatting with a good friend over a spicy yet soothing cup of tea. Interspersed with the laughter and reminiscences are support and encouragement that help the reader create a more spontaneous and authentic life. We are encouraged to recognize and celebrate our personal growth and wisdom while we still pay attention to those areas in our lives that may need a little spit and polish.

As I read through each section I was reminded that older women are truly blessed today. Never before have older women enjoyed so much opportunity to continue our mental, emotional, and spiritual growth. We're living longer, healthier, more productive lives and though we may no longer be as young in body, many of us are actually much younger in attitude than our earlier selves. We know that having moved through the first two stages of our lives, we've earned the right to a little creative selfishness—the right to dance to a different drummer, make our own decisions, live out our neglected dreams, speak our truth, and unabashedly embrace both joy and sorrow.

The author also encourages us to fulfill our roles as wise older women (WOWs) and to use our knowledge and experience to mentor the young women and men in our lives. Through our example they can learn that self-appreciation and unconditional love for ourselves only strengthens our ability to love and support others.

Freedoms After 50 is a wonderful gift for those special WOWs in your life and a great read for any of us who want to "sage as we age." I'm sure that readers will find their own experiences mirrored on these pages.

—Sandra Martz, editor of *When I'm An Old Woman I Shall Wear Purple*

Introduction
Freer Today Than Yesterday

Wouldn't it be wonderful if each night before falling asleep we could truthfully say to ourselves, "Today I was freer than I was yesterday"? Free from fears, free to be uniquely ourselves, free to say what we mean and mean what we say, free to genuinely enjoy and celebrate life. Being a child of the 1940s and 50s, I feel as if I didn't actually wake up to the possibility of personal freedom until my early thirties. As most wake-up calls are, mine was precipitated by a huge crisis—a divorce. Like the pain produced by a giant cattle prod, that crisis jolted me into taking my first halting steps toward freeing myself from "the rules" that I had allowed to limit my life and my choices.

It wasn't until I turned forty that I decided it might be fun and helpful to have a motto for each remaining decade. That year I chose "Forty is feisty." For the fifties, my motto is "Fifty is freedom," and I have found it to be mainly true. Probably the most significant freedom that I'm experiencing is a sense of empowerment that enables me to speak my mind and stand up for my rights and desires. And I have noticed this same ability coming to the fore in a great number of my women friends. Perhaps it comes from an increased awareness of our inherent strength, an expanded sense of self-worth, and a willingness to take risks. I'm not sure of the exact reasons but, for many of us, empowerment and honesty seem to be an upside of the aging process.

When the time comes to create a motto for my next decade (just the blink of a gnat's eyelash away), I'm thinking of "Sixty is serendipitous." Serendipitous brings to mind spaciousness, enthusiasm, angel feathers, and fun—each of which I would gladly welcome into my life at any time. For the following decades, how about "Seventy is sagacious," "Eighty is exciting," and "Ninety is nifty"? I hope that such mottoes will encourage me to keep my arms and heart open toward myself and in cele-bration of womanhood in general as we create new tem-plates for our lives—who we are, what we can do, and what we can become as we greet the cycles of aging.

I want you to know that the freedoms on the follow-ing pages are ones that I aspire to, not ones I've totally mastered. It's true that for hours at a time, and some-times even days and weeks, I can feel these freedoms in my heart, gut, and life. But sometimes those dragon voices—Doubt and Fear—breathe fire on my self-confi-dence, melting it down into unrecognizable goop. When this happens, I need a friendly reminder to put me back on track, which is one reason why I wrote this book. I hope it will become a friend for you too.

Happily, I've discovered that for me one of the benefits of aging is maturity and a deep trust in my ability to regain my equilibrium quickly when I'm knocked off kilter. Consequently, my sense of self-worth is more resilient than when I was younger and rarely, if ever, dissolves beyond repair and renewal. I imagine the same is true for you. I am so thankful for this ability to rebalance and believe it's one of the most wonderful freedoms that we can attain as the years march by.

Through experience and commitment, we WOWs (Wise Older Women) have earned the right to live *our own* lives, have given ourselves permission to laugh heartily and cry easily, have laced our lives with gracious acceptance, and have advanced our ability to love unconditionally. In addition, we women have also been intrepid explorers. Practically from the cradle, we have accepted the challenge of clearing a path through the tangle of societal limitations toward increased freedom and fairness. As with any new passage, this freedom trail needs consistent planting and pruning. I believe we're up to the task. Our sacred trust is to implement and increase the freedoms we now find ourselves gleaning, for the thriving of our children, our families, and our planet depends upon equitable freedom for each and all.

I hope that *Freedoms After 50* will not only act as a catalyst for increasing your individual sense of freedom but will also lighten your heart and give you a few chuckles and smiles of recognition along the way. Please enjoy it, and while reading congratulate yourself on the wisdom and whimsy that you are gathering through the years.

After fifty, I am free to . . .

Laugh at Forgetfulness

Fleeting thoughts skimming
Across the lake of my mind
Skipping, skipping . . .
      gone

Around our house, conversations between my husband and me often sound like this: "Gene, honey!"
"Yes?"
(Pause)
"Oh rats! I don't have a clue!"
(Empathetic laughter)
Between my office and Gene's there seems to be a black hole that impishly sucks ideas directly out of my head and drops them into a bottomless lake, never to be seen again. I've learned that it is best to deal with this situation in a lighthearted manner.

Although it's true that our foibles and frustrations—not the least of which is forgetfulness—seem to increase as the years go by, so does our ability to laugh at them, thank goodness.

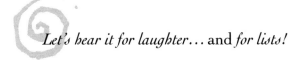

Let's hear it for laughter . . . and for lists!

Roll with the Punches

A dear friend and I were talking about the quiet joy we feel over our burgeoning ability to greet almost all circumstances with equanimity. Laughing, we decided that is probably the reason why our once-youthful, firm bottoms now look less like basketballs and more like the sand-filled bases of those clown punching balloons that were popular when our kids were young.

Age is reforming our bodies to better roll with the punches!

Realize That Attitude Is Everything

Albert Einstein once said, "There are only two ways to live your life. One is as though nothing is a miracle. The other is as though everything is a miracle." I couldn't agree more. It is not circumstances that dictate how we feel, act, and even look; it is attitude. Having an optimistic, loving, and heartfelt attitude toward life means that we will have a *better* life, no matter what hand we are dealt.

Even if we are dedicated downers, choosing to live from the HEART can help us create an upbeat attitude. When we can

H — Honor ourselves and others
E — Be Enthusiastic and Encouraging
A — Appreciate everything and everyone
R — Respect all forms of life, nature, and property
T — Trust that we are loved and lovable

we'll find that both our attitude and our mood will elevate.

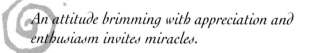

An attitude brimming with appreciation and enthusiasm invites miracles.

Eliminate Angst

Angst is defined as "a gloomy, often neurotic feeling of anxiety and depression"—something we can well do without. Eliminating angst doesn't mean that we won't have pain and grief or be discouraged and disappointed at times. We will. Such feelings are part of the human experience, and growing through them is a large part of the maturation process.

Being afflicted by angst, however, stunts our growth and magnifies pain exponentially. If you are normally angst-free, congratulate yourself. If plagued by habitual angst, please do yourself the life-enhancing favor of finding help. Angst is a habit that can be broken.

Graceful aging is graced by an absence of angst.

Honor My Wrinkles

Whenever I look at photographs of weathered elders, I think "Look at that beautiful face" or "Each of those wrinkles was etched by experience. How I'd love to hear the stories she could tell." However, I'm finding it harder to look in the mirror and think such sweet thoughts about my own face. So, in order to view my winkles and sags more gently, I've created the WOW (Wise Older Women) club. The club's only mission is to honor aging. So far, the membership is quite small, but I'd love for you to join me.

As a good club member, when I stand, semi-aghast, in front of the mirror, I try to reframe my negative thoughts into honoring ones, such as, "Look at the softness of my body. How great it is for hugging and lapsitting." Or I may remark "The melting of my jawline is symbolic of the mellowing of rigid and judgmental patterns and beliefs." Although these statements are definitely rationalizations, they are also true. And WOW! They sure make me feel better.

As Wise (and Wrinkled) Older Women, we can become models and mentors for the generations to follow.

Speak My Truth

In her later years, poet May Sarton once noted: "It always comes back to the same necessity: go deep enough and there is a bedrock of truth, however hard." One of the empowering commitments we Wise Older Women can make is to discover our unique truth in any given moment and then either share it constructively or remain silent, not because we *have to*, but because we *choose to*.

In the Great Wheel of Life, an ancient circular symbol used by native cultures for thousands of years, one of the Four Noble Truths is:

TELL THE TRUTH without blame or judgment. Say what you mean and mean what you say.
or
KEEP NOBLE SILENCE. From an empowered position, choose to remain silent without resentment or bitterness.

This wise guideline helped me realize that there is often nothing at all noble about my silence. But it is also teaching me that it's perfectly all right to gently speak my truth even when doing so is very difficult.

Choosing to honor our truth is choosing to honor our authentic selves.

Trash Judgment

Judgment, the offspring of fear, ignorance, and expectations, is definitely a habit worthy only of the dump. A few of the synonyms for trash are filth, debris, rubbish, and waste, none of which are desirable as collectibles.

Although we women usually reserve our most severe criticism and censure for ourselves, judgment has a tendency to get out of control, to slop over, and to contaminate both giver and receiver. In order to change our judging behavior, we need to gently and lovingly gather the courage to face our fears, bring understanding to those areas in which ignorance lingers, and temper our expectations. For, as we judge ourselves, we will surely judge others.

Judgment is trash. Let's toss it away.

Give Up False Humility

Don't toot your own horn.

Smart girls know when to act dumb.

What gave you such a big head?

Boys won't like you if you're too smart.

The meek shall inherit the earth.

Pride goeth before a fall.

The nail that stands up tall is the one that gets hit.

Did any of these proverbial prickly thorns or ones similar to them overrun your garden of life? Sure did mine. It's high time we uproot these nasty weeds and put the false humility they helped create in the compost pile.

 *Damn, I'm good!*

Find My Spiritual Home

One of the most significant freedoms of midlife is the opportunity to pursue spiritual beliefs and practices that feed our souls. Whether we are happily ensconced in a spiritual home or have rebelled against religiosity in one form or another, our spirit-whispers are never completely silent. Quietly but persistently the still, small voice within invites us to dance toward ever-evolving spiritual maturity.

As women over fifty, we have the right and responsibility to embrace the spirituality that resonates with our hearts while allowing others to follow what speaks to theirs.

Each of us is empowered to drink from the cup of spirituality that quenches her own thirst.

Sprout Soul Seeds

Each soul comes into this world carrying a little packet of seeds, unique and individually mixed just for it. Within these soul seeds resides the mystery of our life's purpose. As we plant our seeds in the fertile soil of our experience, nourish them with awareness, and tend them with commitment, they flower into the creativity with which we are called to bless both ourselves and others.

Emulating the plant kingdom, some of our seeds bloom early, while others are formulated to bring color into our later years. You have already grown many seeds to fruition—perhaps those of teacher, scientist, mother, artist, healer. Grounded now in the wisdom and ingenuity you've gleaned over the years, what seeds still yearn to blossom within you and bring beauty to the world? It doesn't matter what it is. As long as it is truly your own soul seed, it will be complete and right.

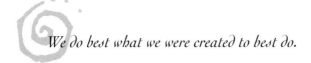

We do best what we were created to best do.

Transform the Hideous Holiday Hag

Right up front I'd better admit that I'm a holiday junkie, one of the only people I know who says "yea" instead of "yuck" when Christmas decorations go up before Halloween. I love even the corniest aspects, most notably the day when the local shopping-mall Santa poses with people and their pets.

For many years, however, my love affair with the holidays was more of a fatal attraction. In those trying-to-be-perfect-times, I was the Hideous Holiday Hag swept into an abyss of obligation and overwhelm. Because I wanted to do each tiny thing absolutely right, everything became a hassle. Only two aspects of the holiday season remained heartful to me: Christmas Eve church service and Christmas morning filled with my children's excitement.

What transformed the Hideous Holiday Hag? The answer is so simple that I'm almost embarrassed to write it. I remembered. I remembered that Thanksgiving is about gratitude and that Christmas honors the energy of Love ushered into the world by a God who cared and still does. I remembered to simplify, simplify, simplify. And I remembered to make a commitment to remain centered in my heart as much as possible.

By remembering the essence of the holidays, we can more easily enjoy them in a heartful way.

Weigh What's Comfortable

Who among us doesn't have an issue or two about weight? I certainly do. Over the years, I figure I've lost about 2,000 pounds. As of today, all of them have been found.

But through the following conversation with myself, I had a little breakthrough on the subject while trying on clothes recently.

"Darn, this makes me look chubby!"

"You *are* chubby, m'dear, grandma chubby. You love the material and comfort of this outfit, so buy it."

It has turned out to be one of my favorite garbs, and I try—with fairly frequent success—to feel *soft* in it, not chubby.

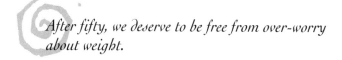

After fifty, we deserve to be free from over-worry about weight.

Accept Responsibility Without Blame

Don't blame, don't shame, don't play the game.
—Carol Parrish

To keep a firm hand on the helm of our own ship, we need to accept responsibility for all aspects of our lives. Not taking responsibility abandons us to the mercy of each stray wind, storm, and piece of floating debris within and around us. Buffeted, bucking, turning, twisting—out of control.

However, and it is a *big* however, it's crucial that we don't burden responsibility with the onus of blame. We will make mistakes, do things poorly, and be less than wonderful once in a while, and we need to take responsibility at those times. But that doesn't mean we should assign blame to ourselves or others. Shaming ourselves with blame only punishes us for taking responsibility and causes us to hesitate to do so again.

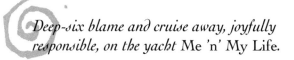

Deep-six blame and cruise away, joyfully responsible, on the yacht Me 'n' My Life.

Meander and Savor Rather Than Scurry and Gulp

God did not create hurry.

—Finnish proverb

Do you remember front porches or side yards furnished with comfy swings, gliders, or rocking chairs? As a kid I spent untold number of hours "doing nothing" in our front porch swing. I often went there to be comforted by the rocking rhythm when I was experiencing sadness or pain. In that swing I savored both solitude and solace. Luckily, I had other places to meander for adventure and exploration, as I imagine you did also.

As children, we intuitively know that meandering and savoring are good for our souls. It is only as adults, besieged by demands on our time and energy, that we succumb to the tendency to scurry and gulp. Let us hope that after we reach fifty, those demands have lessened and we can slow down and let our souls catch up with our bodies.

Let us once more meander and savor the sweetness of life.

Get Out of an Overheated Kitchen

There is a lot of truth in the old cliché: "If you can't stand the heat, get out of the kitchen." Although we've been taught to tough it out when the temperature rises to an uncomfortable degree in our relationships, occasionally it's simply wiser to run away.

A woman I know had used up her allotment of marital verbiage trying to get her husband to understand the subtle—and not so subtle—ways that he put her down. Nothing seemed to get through to him, and as a result she was worn down to the point of depression. I encouraged her to stop talking and to tell him that the next time he behaved disrespectfully she would silently leave. He did and she did. (A very nice hotel was her destination.) Her temporary departure turned out to be exactly the jolt he needed, and I'm happy to report that their kitchen is now comfortably cooler.

At times it is exceedingly wise to exit expeditiously.

Can Perfectionism

Remember the adage "Anything worth doing is worth doing right"? But what is right, and who is determining the definition? Does right mean flawless or perfect? If so, we're doomed to failure because it is impossible to be perfect. Expecting perfection of ourselves breeds a fear of failure, and fear of any kind chokes our ability to love — ourselves and those around us.

I've certainly been known to bludgeon myself black and blue with the perfection pole, but I received a valuable lesson one day while helping my son paint the interior of his house. Very concerned, I wailed, "Oh, Mike, I've gotten all sorts of little smears on the ceiling!" He came sauntering in, glanced casually at my imperfect work, and said, "Oh, Mom, relax. It looks great compared to how it was. It's good enough!"

Good enough... What a beautiful phrase. The rest of our painting time was a laugh- and love-filled story-fest. Free of the need to please him with perfection, I was able to let love pour through.

Being who we are and doing what we do with love is what's really important. If things turn out perfectly once in a while, hallelujah! If they don't, oh well.

Anything done with love is good enough.

Forgive with Abandon

Because no one is perfect, each of us needs to forgive and be forgiven.

Imperfect actions are spawned from fear, and although we may never condone certain behaviors, true forgiveness includes total acceptance of ourselves and others as people trying to do their best. Only when bathed in an aura of acceptance can we feel safe enough to face our fears, heal our wounds, and invite happiness back into our lives.

Therefore, may understanding guide our hearts and compassion our words as we move from the land of fear into the realm of forgiveness. It's crucial to remember that we should be the first recipients of our own forgiving love and acceptance. Sometimes not easily done, but essential, nonetheless.

Love-in-action throws open its accepting heart and forgives with abandon.

Grace Each Moment with Gratitude

Nothing lasts forever. Neither joy nor sorrow. And because each emanates from the precious gift of life, every moment, no matter how dark or light, is a moment worthy of gratitude.

To fill our lives with grace, we need to kiss our joys as they fly gently to our hearts, and, equally important although much more difficult, we also need to accept and give thanks for sorrows that shroud our hearts. Giving thanks for the sadness and pain is more easily done when we explore what our soul can learn from the experience.

When we freely use the wisdom acquired over the years to give thanks in all things, sorrows flee more quickly, joy is a daily guest, and growth is inevitable.

Gracing each minute with gratitude fills our hearts to overflowing.

Expect Respect

An excerpt from a 1950s home economics textbook that advises high school girls about their role in marriage is making the e-mail rounds. In part, admonishments for her behavior on her husband's daily return from work include "Prepare yourself: Take 15 minutes to rest so you will be refreshed when he arrives. Touch up your makeup, put a ribbon in your hair and be fresh looking.... Make him comfortable: Suggest he lie down in the bedroom and arrange his pillow for him...." and "Listen to him and never complain." I remember that book! Do you? At the time, I swallowed its message hook, line, and sinker.

Many of us over-fifty women, "educated" from those very same textbooks, were taught that everyone else was worthy of respect and pampering and that we were the ones to offer it, *not* receive it. Is it any wonder that learning to require respect is often a challenge for us? But with the wisdom born of maturity, we can *un*learn lopsided rules and embrace fair and equitable ways of relating.

I expect to be treated with respect and accept nothing less.

Live Gently with Myself and Others

With maturity,
the sweeter the rose
the softer the thorns.

Gentle actions and gentle attitudes provide an oasis in the harsh reality of our fast-paced, often impersonal society. What a balm it is to be greeted with gentle concern and soft hugs when our hearts are bruised.

Although most of us are gentle with others in times of crisis, are we equally gentle with ourselves? If not, then gentleness is a virtue in need of cultivation. In a climate of gentleness, we feel safe — safe to set aside our shields of protection and invite love to flow freely through and from us.

Enriching our ability to live gently with ourselves and others creates a cascade of good feelings, sweet kindness, and loving connections within and around us. Sheltered by a caring ambiance such as this, each of us can better flourish and flower.

Living gently is a blessing we can bestow daily.

Take Separate Vacations

We sometimes get the message that it is verboten in long-term relationships to do things separately. Not true. We are not clones of our loved ones, and they are not clones of us. In fact, very often we derive growth and relaxation from totally different sources.

While it's fun and bonding to do things together, it is also exciting and adventurous to go off on our own. Doing so gives us the opportunity to bring back rich experiences and added vitality to our relationship.

Heigh ho, Heigh ho, it's off alone I go ...

Sort and Cull What Mother Always Told Me

My mother was a wonderful woman whom I loved dearly, and most of the tidbits she taught me have been valuable assets as I trek along my path. But we've come down the road a ways since Mother's time and there are a few philosophic thistles, learned at her knee, that I'm still trying to pry from my belief system.

The burr that springs to mind is "A man may work from sun to sun, but a woman's work is never done." I cannot tell you what impact this little sentence has had (and *still* has, I admit with a heavy sigh) on my ability to relax, both day and night. In sorting and culling inner adages, I finally edited this one to read, "A man may work from sun to sun and therefore so can you, Hon." You can imagine how delighted I am when daylight saving time causes the sun to hang around until all hours of the night!

As we become the dispensers of wisdom, it's important to treasure the gems we learned but discard the barbs.

Treat Health as Wealth

Native American teacher White Eagle once said, "Be compassionate and refrain from any condemnation or criticism because these are the emotions which sow seeds of disharmony in the physical body. Take care, be kind to your sister body, who is your servant and needs your love and your wisdom."

As White Eagle's teaching reveals, caring for our body encompasses not only what we do with it and what goes into it but also those thoughts that emanate from it. All are vital for maintaining and enjoying abundant health.

It's important for us to treat our bodies well, for unlike a little sea critter that can find a new home when its old shell is broken, we can't exchange one body for another. Our body is the one and only vehicle that we have for fully sensing and appreciating this wondrous human experience. Therefore, it is a treasure beyond compare—ours to value, treat gently, and protect.

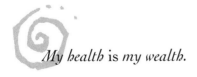

My health is *my wealth.*

Dump the Toad of Overload

There is a funny definition circulating on the Internet that defines a Salmon Day as "swimming upstream all day only to get screwed in the end."

All of us can probably identify with that skewered feeling, at least occasionally. One of the best ways to feel taken advantage of is to become a slave to the odious Toad of Overload. And it's frighteningly easy to do. Here's how. Simply say *yes* more than you feel like, do more than you're comfortable with, give more than you receive, and create unrealistic deadlines for yourself. Shazam! The Toad deftly drops a choke chain around your neck, which is often accompanied by discouragement and a weariness deeper than bone.

As we age and sage, let's dump the toad and teach the salmon a few new tricks. Saying no *and swimming* with *the current are two good starters.*

Mimic Feline Friends

I prefer cats to dogs. Admitting that almost feels like a crime against apple pie and motherhood. Actually, it wasn't until I was close to fifty that I figured out why I favored felines. I was uncomfortable around dogs because they reminded me of *myself*—overly eager to please, furiously wagging tails hoping for a pat on the head, pitifully appreciative of any attention, and terrifically loyal. All of these qualities can be wonderful, of course, but it is definitely healthier to balance them with a few self-assured cat qualities.

Given my insight, isn't it interesting that dogs are called man's best friend. Although, I have no trouble with being my man's best friend, I have no desire to ever again be overly needy or, heaven forbid, to roll over and play dead as I was apt to do when I was younger.

To break some self-defeating habits, I am learning to mimic feline friends.

Cook As Little As Possible

52

I know that there are people who love to cook, but when Goddess created woman, she gave some of us the resources to cheerfully prepare only 1,000,003 obligatory meals. When those have been provided, this particular type of over-fifty woman can either choose to cook for pleasure or take pleasure in *not* cooking.

Some women are incredibly lucky or were exceedingly clever in training family members, and therefore have cooking partners. If you are one of them, I congratulate you for establishing this treasure in your freedom chest. Shortsightedly, I was totally remiss in creating any chefs other than myself; but out of necessity over the past several years, my husband has become a very inventive forager who has never missed a meal.

There are many times now, sometimes even without guilt, when I grant myself the freedom to assert my non-cooking credo of "Forage, Take Out, or Take Me Out." Why not give it a try?

Pay Attention

A wise Hawaiian shaman once taught me a valuable lesson by saying, "Sue, all of the wisdom that I have to give you can be summed up in two words: Pay attention."

Pay attention and we evolve as we are meant to evolve. Pay attention and our loved ones receive the nurturing they desire. Pay attention and we are truly present in the moment. Pay attention and our hearts expand. Pay attention and God appears closer and mysteries become clearer.

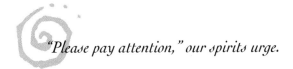

"Please pay attention," our spirits urge.

Develop a Positive Naptitude

There is wonderful snooze news afoot in a book entitled *The Art of Napping* by William Anthony, a Boston University professor. The author notes that most Americans are sleep-deprived, a condition detrimental to both our intellect and our health. Maybe that's why we get so cranky and stressed out. Like little kids, we need our naps.

Famous nappers like Albert Einstein and Winston Churchill can inspire us, but probably our best coaches are stretched out or curled up in a patch of sun right in our own homes. Pets are admirable nappers, able to doze off whenever the mood strikes. After fifty, it's wonderfully healthy for us to follow the example of both the famous and the four-pawed and recharge ourselves through regular napping.

For the good of my body and brain I am developing a positive naptitude.

Act on My Intuition

Although the term *crone* is defined by Webster as an ugly, withered old woman or an old hag, earlier definitions were more complimentary. Crones were considered wise women because they retained their lunar "wise blood" rather than shedding it each month. Deeply attuned to their intuition, older women emanated love as they acted from their innate knowingness. Trusting the truth of their intuition, crones were unafraid to give counsel to those who sought their guidance.

And so it is with us, whether we recognize it or not. We are crones, women whose hearts resonate with intuition that flows from an ancient and dependable wellspring within us. After fifty, this wisdom-source implores us to honor, appreciate, and act upon our intuition as much—or even more—as we do on our intellect.

Intuition is a heart message minus the static.

Dust Others Lightly with Love

Sometimes our love can become heavy-handed, bogged down by attachment, worry, and obligation. How much better it is when we offer our love lightly, as if playfully sprinkling fairy-dust upon those we care about!

Easily said, not easily done, but definitely worth the effort. My adult children, especially, much prefer being dusted with love rather than slathered with gooey and guilt-provoking over-care.

Let us love softly, lightly, with open hands and open hearts.

Give Away My Services

I love the passage from the Gospel of Matthew that tells us to "heal the sick, cleanse the lepers, cast out demons; freely you have received, freely give." It helps me remember that individually, we are like small lakes. When there is both an inflow and egress, the water remains fresh and clean. But when a lake has no outlet, the water is trapped and becomes stagnant and covered with scum. The same is true for us. When energy is welcomed and accepted within us and then invited to flow from us in the service of others, we remain clear and vibrantly alive.

Allowing energy to flow through us attunes us to the Law of Generosity: *That which is freely given away returns manyfold*. Energy-returns are often experienced as light-heartness, a sense of accomplishment, a feeling of being worthwhile, and the knowledge that we have been useful to a person, an activity, or a cause.

We are freshwater beings, born to give generously and joyously.

Write Bad Poetry and Worse Haiku

One of the privileges and responsibilities of middle age is to bring forth our creativity more fully. For me, that is best done in poetry. Although I've sprinkled words on pages since I was very young, I'd always been intimidated by "real" poetry until a wonderful friend, who is an English teacher, helped change my attitude by defining poetry as "eliciting or explaining feelings in a concise and simple manner." We can all play with doing that.

The Japanese haiku is especially simple because there is a formula to follow: 3 lines of 5, 7, and 5 syllables, respectively, using a nature theme. I wrote the following haiku when our family was going through some turmoil over religious differences:

> Wolves together stand
> howling soft and loud at light,
> singing family songs.

I still find reciting or singing this little haiku comforting when my family is in a discombobulated state.

Let your mind and heart dance to the rhythm of creativity, however you express it.

Relinquish the Worry Habit

My mother was the reigning Queen of Worry, and I was her Apprentice Princess. Especially during my twenties and thirties, I was good at it. Darn good! And tired, darn tired. By the time I hit my forties, I was so worn out and bored by my worry habit that I decided it was high time to give it up. Easier said than done. But I was determined.

Worry is a negative affirmation. Realizing that, I tore up my Princess of Worry card and became very dutiful about replacing worrisome thoughts with prayers, positive affirmations, even repetitive chants when necessary. Admittedly, the process was slow going but now, in my fifties, I am generally able to abdicate the throne of worry.

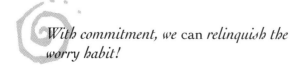

With commitment, we can *relinquish the worry habit!*

Cultivate Kindness

People ask me about my religion. My religion is very simple. My religion is kindness.

—His Holiness the 14th Dalai Lama

After hearing the Dalai Lama speak at the University of Colorado, my son, with superb understatement, said, "He's an appealing gentlemen, isn't he!" Absolutely. It was actually a wonderful adjective to describe his energy and attitude, and the world would be a far better place if we all religiously adopted similar attributes. His Holiness emanates sweetness and optimism. Because of his philosophy and the leadership that accompanied it, this amiable and humble man was awarded a Nobel Peace Prize in 1989.

As we cultivate kindness toward ourselves and others, we personally award small but noble peace prizes each day.

Choose Gracious Acceptance

Gracious acceptance means giving up sharp-edged resistance to things that don't go our way and choosing to substitute a softly accepting attitude. It's a better choice for ourselves and our companions because then we don't spend time bitterly wishing for things to be different or complaining about what is.

My husband, Gene, shared the concept of gracious acceptance with me during a long-anticipated Florida vacation that was marred by torrential rains and ravenous mosquitos. Those two little words—gracious acceptance—made a profound difference in our enjoyment of each other in an otherwise disappointing situation.

One of the joys of maturity is realizing that it's perfectly all right to give up trying to control everything and accept what is. What a blessed relief!

With gracious acceptance, we can float like leaves on the current of life.

Celebrate the Differences Between Men and Women

It's no big surprise that, yes, the genders are different. And those differences can drive us crazy—until we learn to enjoy each other *because of* and not *in spite of* them.

It might be easier to celebrate the contrasts between us if we imagined ourselves and the men in our lives as uniquely different spices blended into the same broth. Sometimes, I'll grant you, our inherent differences do put us "in the soup" with each other.

In or out of the soup, one of the most valuable contributions that we Wise Older Women can make to our beleaguered world is to foster peace within ourselves, our homes, and communities. Where better to start than by waving a white flag in the so-called war between the sexes?

It would be great if we held a banner high for each gender proclaiming, "Let's celebrate each other!"

Respect My Need for Security

A woman's sense of well-being is directly proportional to her sense of security. Maybe this need was imprinted onto the very cells of our collective psyches long ago, when fierce saber-toothed tigers lurked hungrily outside our caves. Whatever the cause, be it fear of saber-toothed saliva or, more likely, an instinctive need to protect our babies, we women *naturally need* security.

Security and stability bring peace of mind. I know that I am happiest and most productive when I feel secure in all areas—physical, emotional, mental, and spiritual. Of course, it isn't always possible to *be* secure in outward circumstances, but it is usually possible to *feel* secure. In order to survive those times when outward security seems iffy at best, I try my darndest to create a bedrock of security within me by anchoring myself to the spiritual truth that God loves me, all is well, and I am safe.

During life's storms, how do you make yourself feel safe and secure?

Ask for What I Want and Need

Imagine for a minute that we are standing at the Pearly Gates presenting our life's ledger to Saints Peter and Priscilla. Across the top are two column headings:

1. Giving others what they want and need

2. Asking for (and getting) what I want and need

My bet is that no matter how adept she becomes at asking for what she wants and needs, at the end of her life, a typical woman's ledger will be overbalanced in favor of number one.

I've heard it rumored, via the Pearly Gate vine, that the saints actually admire symmetrical records.

Be My Own Authority

As young women, many of us abdicated our authority, thinking that others (especially men) were smarter than we and, therefore, able to make better decisions for us. A very important task of midlife is to reclaim our authority. As we own the reality that we are the one and only expert concerning our own lives, we will have the courage to make our own choices, honor reasonable limits and boundaries, live in our own way, and set our own priorities.

As with all growth, assuming the mantle of authority is a process. It takes both time and commitment. Be gentle with yourself as you take the steps, no matter how small or gigantic.

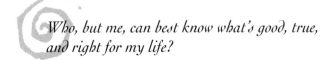

Who, but me, can best know what's good, true, and right for my life?

Put the Martyr in Mothballs

Who of us doesn't have a story about dragging our almost dead bodies out of bed to go to work or to take care of someone at home? Although it happened about thirty years ago, I remember my favorite martyr story as if it were yesterday. Both my babies and I were struck down with the two-ended flu while their father—not my current husband, I hasten to add—jauntily commuted to his office sixty miles away. Luckily, I was too ill for murder.

Recently, I experienced my one and only migraine headache and it became quite apparent that my martyr is safely wrapped in mothballs. Wanly I lay on the couch accepting wet cloths and sympathy. After small mewling moans from me and phone ultimatums from a child or two, my husband and a visiting son insisted that we go to the hospital. Protesting (weakly, I admit), I went. If the headache hadn't been so painful, the experience, itself, would have been quite pleasant!

So long, Martyr.

Twist the Ears of Fear

Judith, a dear friend of mine, had a dream in which she was running away from a powerful, malevolent woman. In the disjointed manner of dreams, she found a hiding place with other people and then suddenly realized that she was by herself in a different hiding place. Alone, she gathered the courage to leap out of her hiding place and grab her stalker's ears. Screaming, "I hate you! I hate you!" Judith twisted the ears of the horrible woman until she fell to her knees in defeat.

As we pondered the meaning of the dream, I asked Judith what the wicked woman represented to her. Without a moment's hesitation, she answered, "Fear!"

In Judith's dream, she personifies the vast majority of women over fifty. Having gained strength and wisdom through facing, surviving, and triumphing over challenges—both major and minuscule—we can usually muster up the gumption to stop running, turn on our pursuer, and twist the ears of fear until it falls to its knees before us.

Conquering fear is perhaps the greatest freedom we can attain for ourselves.

Dodge Other People's Anger

Learning to deal with our own anger is tough enough, so why in the world do we often step in front of another person's? Because we're women, that's why. We've been trained to be rescuers: Pin a bull's-eye on our chest and jump right into the thick of things to make it all better. Well, I don't know about you, but for me jumping into the middle rarely makes things better. More commonly I end up getting slimed by feelings that are not mine.

Enough already! Let's get out of the way. As we move out of range, anger thrown at us will boomerang back to the senders, allowing them to figure out their own feelings. This evading maneuver is an absolutely essential stratagem for after-fifty women who have no more time or energy for handling more than their fair share.

Your anger is yours; mine is mine. I'll deal with mine and dodge yours, thank you very much.

Lose Track of Time

How long has it been since you were so captivated by an activity, endeavor, or person that you totally lost track of time? If it was yesterday or today, Hallelujah!

Each of us needs to love something so intently that while absorbed in it, we slip from the confines of time's prison. In this timeless space, our spirit soars, creativity flows, and our heart sings. We emerge from such a love-fest renewed and revitalized.

If there is nothing in your life right now that feeds your soul and fuels your creative fire, give yourself the life-affirming gift of finding something about which you can be passionate.

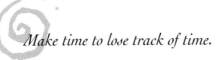

Make time to lose track of time.

Spend a Little Time in the Pity Pit

Sometimes I just want to whine. Like an overheated pig, I yearn to abandon myself to the muck and mud of self-pity, wallowing in it until even my own children wouldn't recognize me. When I can find a companion to sit by the side of my pity pit—fully apprised of his or her role as quiet observer to my tantrum—it often turns out to be a lot of laughs. Given a chance, ardent exaggeration can become hilarious.

It isn't healthy (and it isn't possible) to be a paragon of virtue 100 percent of the time. We need to let our hair down and shake our fists at the gods every now and then. A woman I know, whose life is anything but easy, told me, "I give myself twenty minutes of serious self-pity, and then I stop taking myself so seriously and start working on overcoming whatever is happening." What a great plan.

The trick is not to get stuck in the muck.

Age As Gracefully or Disgracefully As I Choose

Most of us are aging gracefully. We probably never cause friends and families to blush with shame at our antics or to deny that they know us as we career around the circus ring atop an elephant in our fuchsia and turquoise tutu. More's the pity. Now and then, wouldn't it be fun to pepper our lives with a little hot sauce of disgraceful, less than ladylike, behavior?

My mother, a refined and even stoic woman, occasionally indulged in bouts of admirable profanity. It delighted me so much to see her cut loose that I adopted several of her spicy words as my very own. But it was only a couple of years ago that I could give myself permission to use these savory syllables with glee instead of guilt. Although I hope it's not overdone, my tangy talk is now a delicious and disgraceful avenue of expression in which I delight.

What area of your life might you like to flavor ever so slightly with disgrace?

 *Say No*

Being able to use that wonderfully assertive word *no* without guilt, explanation, or remorse is to break free from the prison of obligation. And at our age, we certainly have earned the privilege!

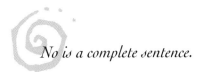

No is a complete sentence.

Delight in Second Childhood

Sometimes dictionaries annoy me greatly. Mine gives second childhood a curt two-word definition: "senile, dotage." Oh, puhleeze! In my opinion, quite opposed to being an era of decline and dotage, a second childhood is replete with redemptive qualities. In the fruitfully free-spirited years after fifty, we have the opportunity to redeem our sense of wonder and awe, reclaim spontaneity and rascality, and consider having fun one of our jobs.

In the service of second childhood, let us dare to become wild and wacky old broads. Let's laugh till we snort, sleep when we're tired, bear-hug our best friends, make up stories, walk barefoot in puddles, find fun in the familiar, break a few silly rules, and *play* house rather than clean house.

In my experience it takes a long time to grow young.

Welcome the Worms

Within the vast reservoir of each of us resides a few dank and slippery bottom-dwellers that occasionally ooze to the surface, causing us to recoil in alarm and clobber them with the nearest weapon.

What might happen if instead of meeting these odious creatures with assault, we invited them to sit beside us on the warm sand, and with a deep desire to understand, asked them what they wanted and needed from us?

Worms of any kind can only transform in the warm light of love and acceptance.

Enjoy My Grandchildren

Right off the bat, the titles are a giveaway. *Grand*child. *Grand*parent. And it gets even better with each successive generation: *Great grand*child. *Great grand*parent. Why is grandparenting so great? Why do we often enjoy our grandchildren as we may never have enjoyed their parents?

Not being totally responsible is the obvious reason for freely enjoying grandchildren, but below that is the truth that we have garnered much wisdom from our years and are more aware of the miracle of life.

To my great sadness, I realize that as an insecure, scared, and unhappy young mother, I saw my children through lizard lids—opaque inner eyelids that filtered out much of the awe and wonder encircling them. Although the years have dimmed my physical eyesight, my inner vision is clearing, and, consequently, I perceive my two-year-old grandson differently than I did my children. I see the miracle of him, watch for the spirit dancing in his eyes, understand his often wordless wisdom, and bask in his freshness.

From day one, we can choose to have a sacred, mindful relationship with these shining souls who are learning to wear their funny body-suits.

Soften Expectations

Almost every woman I know, myself included, habitually or occasionally expects more of herself than is humanly—and sometimes even superhumanly—possible. These harsh and unrealistic expectations are emotional booby traps that shackle us to feelings of failure and disappointment. In the unforgiving glare of unreasonable expectations, both our real and imagined imperfections are highlighted. Not a pretty sight! Nor a loving and gentle one.

Surely now, in the mellower years following fifty, we have earned the right to round off the sharp edges of unfriendly expectations and replace them with unconditional acceptance and continual emotional support. By softening expectations, we benefit both ourselves and those whom we love.

As our bodies soften, may our expectations follow suit.

Open the Door to Impermanence

When I was in my twenties, a teacher I respected told a room full of students that until we accepted the concept of death—especially our own—we would not truly live. The notion was totally foreign to me, but as I looked around the room, I saw the older people were nodding in agreement. I quickly slammed the door shut on the idea then, but after studying with Elisabeth Kubler-Ross, doing hospice work, and being with family and friends during illness and death, I now understand the wisdom of his remark.

We who welcome the seed, nourish the bud, and birth the blossom know well the cycles of life. Coming, going, ebbing, flowing. Darkness and light, tears and joy. Each appears and eventually passes away. Life is a circle of impermanence, and death is the only certainty it offers. Death will come calling, and we do ourselves a huge favor by using each opportunity to overcome our fear and befriend the inevitable. As we are able to accept the impermanence of life, we become infinitely freer.

Although the process of death is often disturbing (I have certainly left my share of bedsides shaking my fist at God), all of my experience has led me to believe that death itself is simply a gentle change of consciousness.

To die is to fall into the awaiting arms of the Beloved.

Allow Healing to Happen Naturally

Mother mourning dove
Without knowing how deeply
Grieves her fallen egg.

Recently I experienced several episodes of illness,
death, and disappointment in my life. Caught in the
helper, pull-yourself-up-by-your-bootstraps mode, I
wasn't even aware of my own unresolved grief, guilt, and
sense of failure. I seemed to be wading through vanilla
tapioca. Everything was bland and tiring. Enthusiasm
was nonexistent, courage and confidence dwindled, and
creativity was a distant memory.

Interestingly, swimming with dolphins helped me
open my heart to myself and understand the amount of
grief I was carrying. After months of denial, I began the
grieving process by allowing myself the vulnerability of
tears — torrents of tears. Anne Morrow Lindbergh beau-
tifully expresses the process we must go through in order
to heal: "If suffering alone taught, all the world would be
wise. To suffering must be added mourning, understanding, patience, love, openness, and the willingness to
remain vulnerable."

*Grief is a process. When it is patiently allowed,
healing happens naturally.*

Enjoy Post-Menopausal Zest

I once heard a woman say, "You know, older chickens make the best soup!" Because that sounded rather sacrificial to me, I amended it to, "Older chickens lay the best eggs." "Well," a farmer drawled in response to my asking if this was a true statement, "I don't know. Could be. But I do know that older chickens don't cackle as much."

Hum... I think we *do* cackle less and less as we mature. In the quiet, perhaps we are better able to hear the sounds of our potential waiting to be hatched. Life requires that we create, and as we pass the age of possible baby-making, we march into an era where myriad possibilities become vibrantly alive within us. Ideally, this is a time when we have not only the yearning but also the freedom to peck open the shells surrounding our personal creative power and realize our dreams and schemes.

What are some of your dreams? What would add zest to your life? You have the opportunity right now to incubate golden eggs.

Remember, older chickens lay the best eggs.

Recognize That Money Is a Form of Energy Exchange

Money is a popular medium used for swapping merchandise and services, and many women are still learning the fine art of bartering. In fact, expecting to be rewarded commensurate with our worth is one of the hardest lessons we women-of-a-certain-age have to learn. We were trained to serve willingly and without pay—or even thanks, in some cases. Consequently, we have a tendency to give away more energy than we get. But the scales are in need of balancing because, in reality, a fair exchange of goods, energy, and time creates more freedom for all.

Ideally, as we provide energy in the form of service to our family, workplace, or both, we are compensated by an equivalent amount coming back to us: attention, appreciation, and security from our families, and money and other financial and emotional benefits from our work. In order to gain equality for ourselves and our sisters, we must first believe that we deserve an even exchange of energy.

Everyone is happier and healthier when energy income and outgo are balanced.

Accept the Mantle of Wisdom

Because we have been taught to augment everyone's self-worth but our own, one of the hardest things for a woman to do is to bow to her own excellence, kneel in acknowledgment, and accept the mantle of wisdom awaiting her.

Deep within our hearts, there is a wisdom so profound that it can be heard only within the silence and spoken not at all. Such heart-wisdom is revealed through action and attitude, and we are called to accept its mantle for the good of all.

To midwife love into the world, we must wrap ourselves in the warm robe of our unique wisdom.

Tap the Power of Prayer

Irrefutable evidence from scientific research done during the past decade assures us that prayer works. According to Larry Dossey, a medical doctor, author, and foremost authority on the relationship between prayer and healing, there are currently 150 studies being conducted right now on the efficacy of prayer from a distance. Preliminary results from these studies indicate that neither distance nor type of prayer matters. What *does* matter is that the simple act of sending loving regard to others is powerful medicine for both receiver and sender.

Prayer takes as many forms as there are individuals. Prayers may be specific desires, detailed visualizations, unbridled praise, or requests for the highest good of all concerned. Theologians and philosophers alike agree that two of the most powerful prayers we can utter are those expressing gratitude and those voicing the ancient wisdom "Thy will be done."

Tap the power of prayer in ways that resonate with your heart, for the Divine Beloved is more attuned to the sincerity of your heart than to the words of your mind.

Sleep the Way I Like

If you are a sound-sleeping snuggle-bug, this page is not for you. This one was written for those of us who are rudely awakened by waterbed tidal waves when our beloved—better known as the Restless Gigantic Salmon—levitates, turns in the air, and crashes back onto the bed. If there were a Richter scale for such nocturnal waves, they would register about an 8.3.

Some of you may, however, be acquainted with the bed-buddy known as Burrito Boy. He's the one who quietly—or maybe not so quietly—rolls over during the night winding the blankets snugly around himself, leaving his loved one icily clutching a tortilla-sized remnant of cover.

Shall I mention snoring, or should we all just take a moment to fondly think of our own bedmate's endearing little noises?

Shakespeare informed us that "sleep knits up the raveled sleeve of care." Well, if you spend most of your night longing to use those knitting needles for a very different purpose, it's time to make some changes. Sleeping alone is not a sign of a collapsing marriage or a crumbling sex life; it just means you want a good night's rest.

Although it may create some waves, after fifty we can lovingly choose to sleep the way we like.

Kiss Guilt Good-bye

Guilt is a built-in safeguard against wrong action. And if guilt remains a twinge, instead of a tourniquet cutting off our life-force, it is useful for correcting behavior and making amends. Unfortunately, women in general have been socialized to grasp guilt to their bosoms and carry the heavy load throughout eternity and beyond. A maxim emphasizes this point: "Show me a woman without guilt, and I'll show you a man." Sad, but often true.

As she was struggling with guilt over her past "sinful life," Eva dreamt of a beast emerging from the bowels of a boat she was piloting. Then Eva heard an unmistakably clear inner message: "Dance with the beast!" Although she found the message loathsome she did as told, trembling with fear and revulsion. The beast was miraculously transformed, and the dance between them became one of joyous freedom. In waking life, Eva began to tame her feelings of guilt into twinges used as opportunities to forgive the young woman she had been. As in the dream, her life became more joyous.

It's time that we claim the freedom to kiss guilt good-bye.

Ask "Why Not Me?"

In Scott Sparrow's book *Blessed Among Women*, there is a wonderful, true story about Mother Mary appearing to a woman in a parking lot. Awed but puzzled, the woman asked, "Why me? I'm not Catholic." Mary answered, "Why *not* you?"

Faced with both the miraculous and the miserable, we have a tendency to ask, "Why me?" How much more productive it would be if we could give up that query and simply accept that we are deserving of blessings received and, equally important, that we have the strength to grow through the challenges that inevitably come our way.

Why not *each and every one of us?*

*Feel Pretty and Sensual Without the
Need to Look Younger*

Cultivating the art of "mirror avoidance" is sometimes the best way to experience this freedom. I say that only partially in jest. There have been times when I was feeling absolutely adorable and incredibly youthful and sexy when, quite by accident, I happened to catch a glimpse of myself in a mirror. Yipes! Who *is* that?

Such a surprising encounter can be deflating, but is the reflection we see in a mirror the real us? No. It's merely an image of the face and body that we've inherited from our families and earned over the years. The feelings, beliefs, and attitudes within us, which we then reflect out into the world and onto others, actually mirror who we are. When those are beautiful, sensual, thoughtful, youthful, compassionate (add your most cherished qualities to this list), *that* is who we are, no matter how we may appear.

The ageless rainbow of attributes within us becomes the palette from which our persona is painted.

Regain My Virginity

I can hear you scoffing: "Once it is gone, how in the world can you regain your virginity?" Easily; it's a matter of semantics. Although "virgin" is now defined as a woman who has never had sexual intercourse, the original definition was "a woman complete unto herself." I like this interpretation because it offers women the assurance of being whole, whether we are in relationship with men or not.

Using the concept of being complete unto ourselves, we can — no matter what our sexual orientation or activity — regain our virginity. I don't know about you, but I definitely lost my virginity, in both senses of the word, in my first marriage. Not only was I no longer chaste, but I became half (if truth be told, a lot less than half) of a couple. Indeed, I viewed my husband as whole while I, feeling like a partially formed being, just tagged along. Ouch! Now, however, the crone is on the climb and I am dedicated to the process of regaining my virginity.

At the center of our beings, we are all whole and complete unto ourselves.

Vacate Victim Territory

Each of us experiences situations in which it is easy to feel victimized. For our own sense of well-being and peace of mind, to say nothing of our healing and growth, we need to vacate victim territory as quickly as possible. Nothing impedes our progress and dulls happiness quite as effectively as shackling ourselves to a cross planted smack-dab in the middle of victim territory. I know, because I once chained myself to the poor-me-divorce-cross for more moons than I care to recall.

With the help of those who loved me, I eventually dragged myself off the cross. Only then could the healing begin for me and my children. The following proverb helped: *The rose that wilts after six days will become a part of the garbage. After six months, the garbage is transformed into a rose.* I was determined to become a new rose, and although it took longer than six months, healing and transformation did take place.

There will be roses and there will be garbage. With a survivor's perspective, there can always be redemption and the return of roses.

Make Peace with Paradox

In our younger years we often want black or white answers. We feel more secure when ideas and beliefs are safely cubbyholed. But as we grow older and wiser, we come to the mysterious realization that, like it or not, life is packed with paradox. Incongruities abound, contradictions flourish, and ambiguity is an actuality. The trick is to accept it all.

Accepting everything is definitely not an easy task. Although I've lost track of the originator of the statement "Old age is not for sissies," I think it is a valuable reminder that aging includes challenges that can demand great courage and endurance. Paradoxically, adversity and freedom regularly wear a double harness as we advance in years. Thankfully, more often than not, wisdom holds the reins and helps us realize that contrast is crucial for honing our souls.

What a blessing it is when we can courageously accept paradox as an enduring reality of life.

Savor Sensuality and Sexuality

Freed from the fear of conception and the bonds of self-consciousness, we in midlife are better able to savor our sensual and sexual selves, even when we are not partnered. There are countless ways to relish sensuality: touching baby leaves, petting a friendly animal, walking in nature during any season, soaking in a warm bath, snuggling under a soft comforter with a cup of hot chocolate (Ahhhh, chocolate. For me, the most sensual of foods!), and listening to wonderful music, just to name a few.

Optimally, sex embraces sensuality to the fullest and moves even deeper into pleasure and meaning. For those of us in relationship, sex is the gift of our true self to another. It is said that at orgasm we meld not only our energies, but the gifts we've gathered over lifetimes. Sexual love is a sacred and healing act. If we don't have a partner at this time, Dr. Ruth would hasten to assure us that it is perfectly fine, even healthy, to sexually pleasure ourselves.

Contrary to what many of us may have learned while growing up, sensuality and sexuality are *good*, even holy. Therefore, we can feel free to invite the Divine to share our sensuality and be present in both singular and partnered love rendezvous!

Sensuality and sexuality, the spice of life!

Soar on the Wings of Friendship

Lord Byron said, "Friendship is Love without his wings." But I beg to differ; I believe that *Friendship gives Love its wings!*

Our friends provide ballast when we are weathering rough seas; in celebration, they soar with us over the mountaintops. Their love provides safe sanctuaries where we can share all that is within and about us. True friends accept us, chaff and grain alike, and almost more important than anything, they laugh with us. And we do the same for them.

Friend, born of my heart, our bloodline is spirit.

Sage As I Age

Those who sage as they age view aging not as a hardship but, rather, as a precious gift filled with promise and replete with possibilities. We may age graciously into simplicity and love, allowing the power from our sense of well-being to permeate the atmosphere around us, or we may vault into older age revved up and in high gear.

I am thinking of two "elderly" women in the second category who run circles around me. As the years pile up, these two seem to *gather* more energy and enthusiasm. At seventy-four, one woman used her well-earned sagacity to start a new business and teach younger women about the vagaries of the business world. The second woman went back to college, finished her degree at seventy-nine, and is now investigating graduate schools. All of this while continuing to work as an intuitive therapist. Makes me tired just thinking about all that activity, so I imagine that I fall into the first category.

Your heart's desire is to evolve into the best "you" possible. Only you know who that is. But no matter what form saging takes for us as individuals, we all have credited many years of wisdom to our life-account. As we continue to accrue wisdom, we are also called upon to invest our sage-savings for the good of all.

To sage as I age, I choose to use it, not lose it.

Carry One Teacup at a Time

Inundated by the needs of others, I asked one day during a writing meditation how I could best serve God, myself, and those who needed me without feeling so overwhelmed. In answer, I wrote the following: "From the vast river of tears flooding our times, fill only the teacup that you alone can carry. An over-filled vessel is too heavy and cumbersome to move, let alone serve. With only one teacup of tears at a time, you may minister effectively and with grace."

The message helped me realize that my personal teacup was smashed at the bottom of a huge barrel overflowing with heavy concern for others. I was carrying everyone's tears within my own heart and body. Doing so wasn't helping them and was paralyzing me. Mercifully, my memory was jogged by the teacup lesson, and I remembered the concept of compassionate detachment: loving, praying, and being there for people in pain, yes, but allowing God to carry all but a small portion of their tears. A lesson more easily stated than implemented, I know.

We can help ourselves and others more effectively by not leaping in the boiling water with them but by extending a steady and loving hand from the rim of the abyss.

Give the Smiley Face a Rest

When those little yellow smiley faces became popular, I was irritated. They were cute, yes, but something about them grated on me. Ah ha! One day I realized that I saw myself in those ubiquitous grins. Were you trained, as I was, to always wear a pleasant expression no matter how you felt? As plain as day, I can remember my wonderful mother trying to protect me from being too transparent by saying, "Sue, you've got to learn to hide your feelings and not let everything show on your face."

Mother may not have meant that I needed to wear a Cheshire cat grin, but unconsciously I interpreted her cautioning to mean that I needed to smilingly do whatever dance needed to be done in order to make others happy. What a burden I was carrying, and often my face was not an authentic representation of how I felt.

Thanks to those annoying little yellow circles, I'm in the process of freeing myself from the let-me-entertain-you-omnipresent-smile syndrome. And, I confess, I sometimes stick smiley faces on letters. A sign of healing, I'm assuming.

When it feels right, give the smiley face a rest!

Find a Bitch-Buddy

Sometimes we need to share grievances in order to move beyond them. Sage William Shakespeare acknowledged this when he said, "Give sorrow words; the grief that does not speak / Whispers the oe'r fraught heart and bids it break."

For this we need a bitch-buddy, one who can hear our complaints and sorrows compassionately, respond appropriately, and then allow them to fly away from her (and often us, too) as easily as the wind sweeps away the puffies from a fully mature dandelion. (One cardinal rule for a bitch-buddy is that she doesn't judge or hold a grudge against any person about whom we complain.)

Removing negative energy from our systems is important to maintaining our health, for congealed resentment and hopelessness love to create cancer and broken hearts, among other things. Of course, habitual complaining is every bit as unhealthy as holding everything in. But occasional bouts of bitchiness are worthwhile when the goal of grumping is to lance wounds and allow all poisonous thoughts and feelings to flow away. Having emotionally flushed, as it were, we are then able to move back into the clear, clean realms of our hearts.

Grumping can be great for your health.

Harbor Hope

As options and possibilities seem to decrease, hopelessness often increases. That's why it is so important to harbor hope as we age and life sometimes seems to narrow down. Hope is the heart of life. Without it the fire within that wills us to "keep on keeping on" is all but extinguished. As the Dalai Lama says, "Live with hope, for lost hope shortens life."

If we find ourselves in a vast wasteland devoid of hope, the best thing we can do for ourselves is to surround ourselves with those who agree to be hopeful for us until we can once again tap into our own reservoirs of hope and trust. As Rev. Ginger Taylor reminds us, "When we face those toughest of times, when we are sliding down the slippery slope, and we're grasping for handrails of hope, we can seek the company of hopeful people."

Protect hope. Bring it into the harbor of your heart where it is safe from even the severest storms.

Master the Firewalk

This little segment is offered as a tribute to the many women I've met who were required to walk through the fire of abuse as children. I am in awe of their strength and courage. Although their professions run the gamut from minister, cultural anthropologist, therapist, nurse, artist, librarian, and teacher, by far their most admirable accomplishments in my eyes center around how they mother their own daughters.

Even as they work on the arduous task of healing the little girls they once were, the vast majority of these fire-walkers raise their daughters (and their sons) with shining wisdom and compassion. It's as if the fires braved as children have purified their hearts and burned away much of the petty residue that many of us carry.

With heartfelt respect, I salute those of you who are mastering the firewalk of your youth and, with mature wisdom and love, are reaching out to support and guide new generations.

Rewrite Unflattering Labels

There I was at the doctor's office asking the dermatologist, a young woman who looked as if she might emerge from adolescence in a year or so, about the little rough patches on my shoulder and collarbone. At least she had the grace to look sheepish when she answered, "We call them age barnacles." Well, *excuse me!* That label could make a person feel like a moth-balled battleship.

With good humor but great determination, my husband and I decided to erase this unflattering medical diagnosis and rewrite it in a more complimentary vein. We jettisoned several names, including "crone crud" and "fossil fungus" before settling on the new label of "wisdom patina."

Don't believe for a minute that only sticks and stones will break our bones; words can break our spirits. But we can unite and rewrite!

Make Balance and Harmony Priorities

We are beings who require balance and harmony in every aspect of our selves—physical, emotional, mental, and spiritual. Realizing where balance and harmony are needed requires a deep commitment. All change takes effort and desire.

One of the best ways to bring equilibrium into our lives is to intentionally make minute-by-minute, day-to-day choices that invite the harmony of love and serenity into our daily experience. Do a little inventory: Are you nourishing your spiritual, emotional, mental, and physical selves? What about balance within relationships? Are you giving and getting equally? If our lives are to be relaxed, meaningful, and sacred, we want and *need* to live in balance within ourselves, with others, and with circumstances.

Bathed in the serenity of balance and harmony, all facets of our selves flourish.

Balance Self and Service

Somewhat humorously, Al-Anon defines codependents as "people who see *someone else's* life flash before their eyes when they die." But those of us who have been totally unbalanced from giving, giving, giving know that there is nothing funny about the trap of codependence.

To appreciate the art of balancing self and service we can look to Mother Nature as our model. Without fail, she (I love the fact that Mother Nature is a she!) maintains equilibrium between abundant flowering and adequate rest. In the appropriate season, Nature blesses us with beauty and nourishment, and then quietly retreats to her roots to be replenished. Doesn't that sound heavenly?

Using Mother Nature as a guide, we, too, can honor the seasons of our hearts. If, like the majority of us, you are over-balanced in the serving category, cultivate a little selfishness and take time to put yourself first. However, if you have been self-absorbed through depression or victimhood, give yourself the restorative gift of being of service to others.

Whether we give away too much or too little of ourselves, our vitality dwindles. By balancing self and service, we invite the life-force to ebb and flow through us as it was created to do.

Turn My Eyes Toward the Ancients

Indigenous peoples, as well as most Eastern cultures, respect the wisdom that aging brings. These societies consider the advancing years an ideal time for psychological and spiritual growth—a time of great perspective, freedom, and illumination—rather than a time of deterioration.

So as our bodies drift southward, let us turn our eyes and hearts toward the Ancients and revel in the mysteries to be revealed in the years after fifty.

Opening to the wonder and wisdom that aging can bring, we soar into the sacred space of eldership.

Acknowledgments

Deep gratitude wings across the ocean to my friend Bobbie Sandoz and the Hawaiian spinner dolphins, both of whom were instrumental in helping me open my heart and heal the grief that had plunged me into a pit of low self-confidence and no creative energy. This restorative trip was a wisely intuitive gift from my wonderful husband, Gene. Also, heartfelt thanks to the friendly spotted dolphins of the Bahamas who, by their presence in the water with me and in the lucid dreams that followed, have helped me unveil a sense of empowerment within myself greater than any I have known before. Thank you, Gene. Thank you, Bobbie. Thank you to Auntie Es and all the dolphins.

And to my longtime friend Lynn Lunde, thank you for all the laughter and the tears, each hour of your time, and the "gray mask," may it rest in peace.

Much applause to my friends Bonnie, Judith, Vimala, Diana, Sherrie, Chris, Betty, Connie, Paula, Ingrid, Carolyn, Annabelle, Cece, Muriel, and Kim, who are all great hand-holders and encouragement-dispensers.

Without the help and support of all the wonderful people at Conari Press, this project could never have been completed. I value and appreciate all of you, and especially Brenda, Annette, and editor Mary Jane Ryan, who fuels my vision, grants me the freedom to "spew, then review," and ultimately sets the spewage straight. As always, wonderful women, thank you!

About Sue Patton Thoele

Licensed psychotherapist Sue Patton Thoele lives in Boulder, Colorado, with her husband, Gene. She is a mom and grandmother as well as a woman's group facilitator, speaker, and baker of creative birthday cakes, who has recently become enthralled by swimming with free dolphins. Sue is the author of *The Courage To Be Yourself*, *The Woman's Book of Courage*, *The Woman's Book of Confidence*, *The Woman's Book of Spirit*, *Autumn of the Spring Chicken*, *The Woman's Book of Soul*, *Heart Centered Marriage*, and *The Courage To Be Yourself Journal*.

Conari Press, established in 1987, publishes books
on topics ranging from spirituality and women's history
to sexuality and personal growth. Our main goal is to
publish quality books that will make a difference
in people's lives—both how we feel about ourselves
and how we relate to one another.

Our readers are our most important resource,
and we value your input, suggestions, and ideas.
We'd love to hear from you—after all,
we are publishing books for you!

For a complete catalog or to get on our mailing list,
please contact us at:

CONARI PRESS
2550 Ninth Street, Suite 101
Berkeley, California 94710

800-685-9595   Fax 510-649-7190
E-mail Conaripub@aol.com